THE NEW
DAN COATES

EASY PIANO

ENCYCLOPEDIA

Project Manager: Carol Cuellar

Foreword

Dan Coates

One of today's foremost personalities in the field of printed music, Dan Coates has been providing teachers and professional musicians with quality piano material since 1975. Equally adept in arranging for beginners or accomplished musicians, his Big Note, Easy Piano and Professional Touch arrangements have made a significant contribution to the industry.

Born in Syracuse, New York, Dan began to play piano at age four. By the time he was 15, he'd won a New York State competition for music composers. After high school graduation, he toured the United States, Canada and Europe as an arranger and pianist with the world-famous group "Up With People."

Dan settled in Miami, Florida, where he studied piano with Ivan Davis at the University of Miami while playing professionally throughout southern Florida. To date, his performance credits include appearances on "Murphy Brown," "My Sister Sam" and at the Opening Ceremonies of the 1984 Summer Olympics in Los Angeles. Dan has also accompanied such artists as Dusty Springfield and Charlotte Rae.

In 1982, Dan began his association with Warner Bros. Publications - an association which has produced more than 400 Dan Coates books and sheets. Throughout the year he conducts piano workshops nationwide, during which he demonstrates his popular arrangements.

CONTENTS

THE WIND BENEATH MY WINGS

Words and Music by
LARRY HENLEY and JEFF SILBAR
Arranged by DAN COATES

9

3. It might have appeared to go unnoticed
that I've got it all here in my heart.
I want you to know I know the truth:
I would be nothing without you.

From the Motion Picture "ROBIN HOOD: PRINCE OF THIEVES"

(EVERYTHING I DO) I DO IT FOR YOU

Words and Music by
BRYAN ADAMS, ROBERT JOHN LANGE
and MICHAEL KAMEN
Arranged by DAN COATES

Oh, you can't

tell me it's not worth try - ing for. I can't

help it, there's noth - ing I want more. Yeah, I would

WHEN A MAN LOVES A WOMAN

Words and Music by
CALVIN LEWIS and ANDREW WRIGHT
Arranged by DAN COATES

HERO

By
WALTER AFANASIEFF and MARIAH CAREY
Arranged by DAN COATES

From the Motion Picture "POETIC JUSTICE"

AGAIN

By
JANET JACKSON,
JAMES HARRIS III and TERRY LEWIS
Arranged by DAN COATES

Moderately Slow

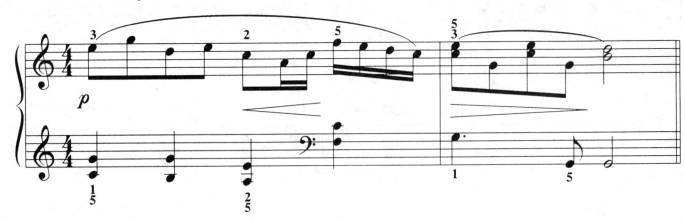

I heard from a friend to-day and she said you were in town. Sud-den-

ly the mem-o-ries came back to me in my mind._____ How can

ALL THE WAY

Words by
SAMMY CAHN

Music by
JAMES VAN HEUSEN
Arranged by DAN COATES

Slowly, with expression

When some-bod-y loves you, it's no good un-less she loves you
When some-bod-y needs you, it's no good un-less she needs you

all the way.

Hap-py to be near you, when you need some-one to cheer you
Through the good or lean years and for all the in be-tween years,

all the way.
come what may.

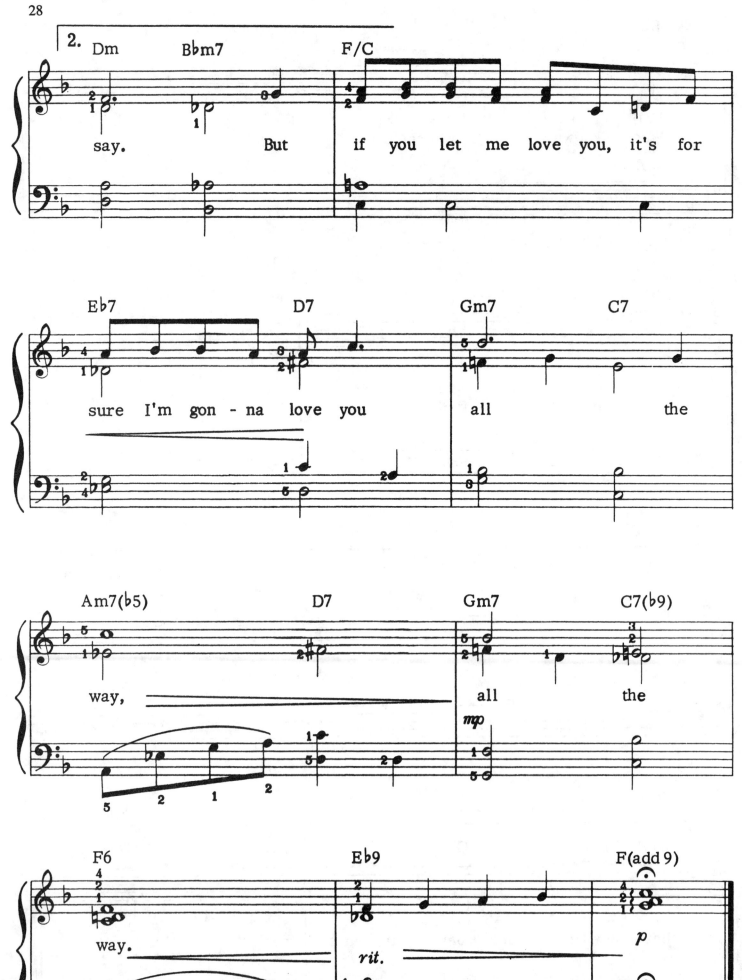

ALWAYS AND FOREVER

Words and Music by
ROD TEMPERTON
Arranged by DAN COATES

1. Al - ways and for - ev - er,_____ each mo - ment with you
2. There'll al - ways be sun - shine_____ when I look at you.

is just like a dream to me that some - how came true.
Some - thing I can't ex - plain, just the things that you do.

And I know to - mor - row_____ will still be the same,
And if you get lone - ly, _____ call me and take

ANOTHER SAD LOVE SONG

By
DARYL SIMMONS and BABYFACE
Arranged by DAN COATES

ANYTHING GOES

Words and Music by
COLE PORTER
Arranged by DAN COATES

In old-en days a glimpse of stock-ing Was looked on as some-thing shock-ing, Now heav-en know, AN-Y-THING GOES. Good auth-ors too who once knew bet-ter words

ANYWHERE THE HEART GOES
(MEGGIE'S THEME)
Based on a Theme from the WARNER BROS. T.V. Movie, "THE THORN BIRDS"

Words by
WILL JENNINGS

Music by
HENRY MANCINI
Arranged by DAN COATES

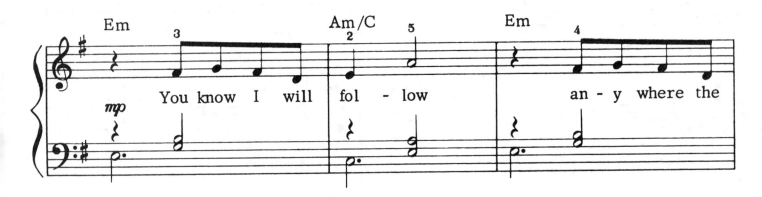

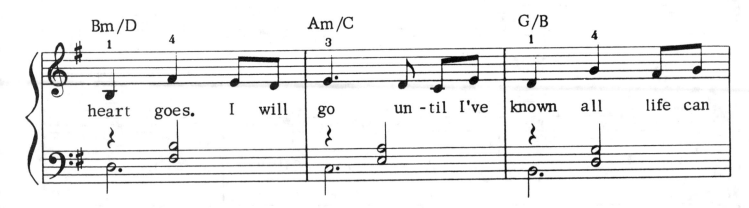

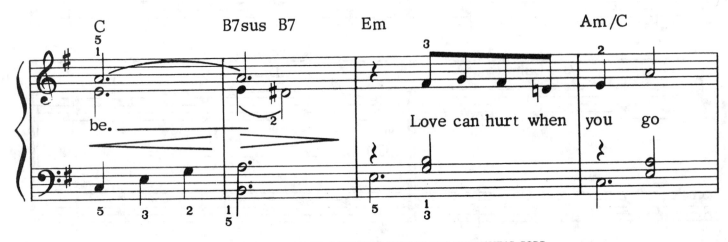

AS TIME GOES BY

Words and Music by
HERMAN HUPFELD
Arranged by DAN COATES

From ''ARTHUR,'' an Orion Pictures Release through Warner Bros.

ARTHUR'S THEME
(Best That You Can Do)

Words and Music by
BURT BACHARACH, CAROLE BAYER SAGER,
CHRISTOPHER CROSS and PETER ALLEN
Arranged by DAN COATES

Moderately

DAYS OF WINE AND ROSES

Words by
JOHNNY MERCER

Music by
HENRY MANCINI
Arranged by DAN COATES

CAN YOU READ MY MIND?
(Love Theme from "SUPERMAN")
A Warner Bros. film

Words by
LESLIE BRICUSSE

Music by
JOHN WILLIAMS
Arranged by DAN COATES

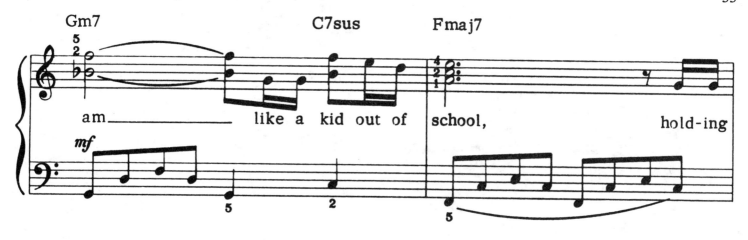

Gm7   C7sus   Fmaj7

am _____ like a kid out of | school,   hold-ing

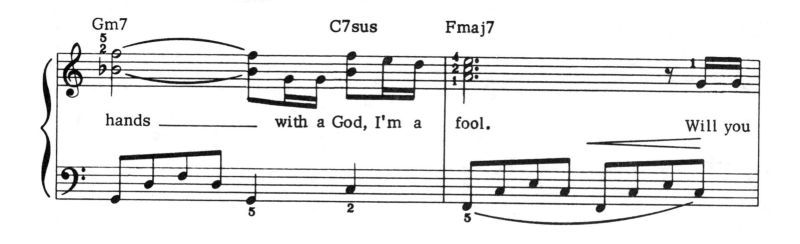

Gm7   C7sus   Fmaj7

hands _____ with a God, I'm a | fool.   Will you

Bb   Ab

look at me quiv-er-ing like a | lit-tle girl shiv-er-ing. You can

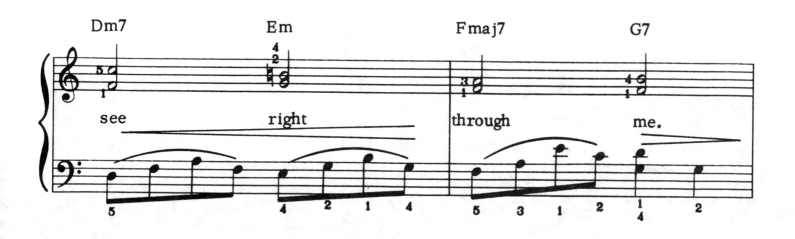

Dm7   Em   Fmaj7   G7

see   right | through   me.

CAN'T FIGHT THIS FEELING

Words and Music by
KEVIN CRONIN
Arranged by DAN COATES

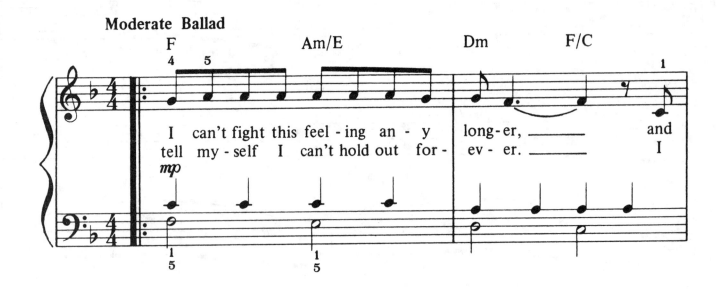

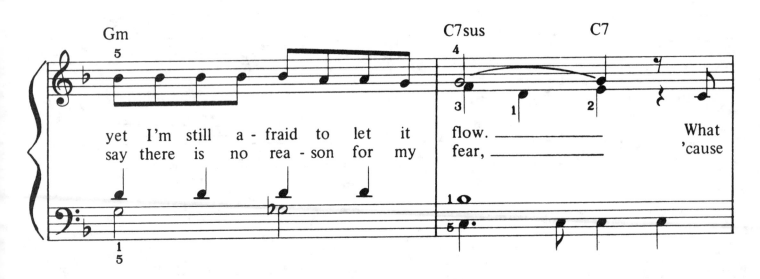

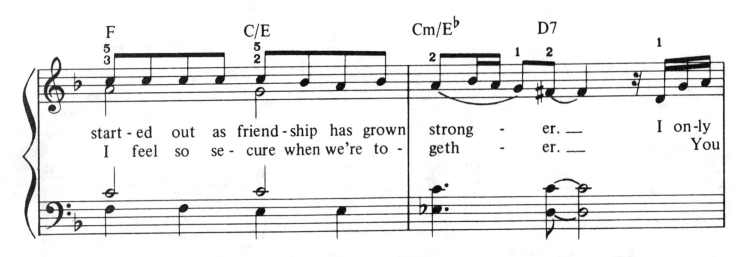

DESPERADO

Words and Music by
DON HENLEY and GLENN FREY
Arranged by DAN COATES

Slowly

Des-per - a - do, why don't you come to your sens - es?__ You been
- a - do, oh, you ain't get-tin' no young-er,__ your

out rid - in' fenc - es for so long now.__ Oh, you're a
pain and your hun - ger they're driv - ing you home.__ And

hard one, I know that you got your rea - sons, these
free-dom, well, that's just some peo-ple talk - in', your

things that are pleas - in' you can hurt you some - how.__
pris - on is walk - in' through this world all a - lone.__

DREAMLOVER

Words and Music by
DAVE HALL and MARIAH CAREY
Arranged by DAN COATES

Moderate, steady beat

EVERGREEN
(Love Theme from "A STAR IS BORN")

Words by
PAUL WILLIAMS

Music by
BARBRA STREISAND
Arranged by DAN COATES

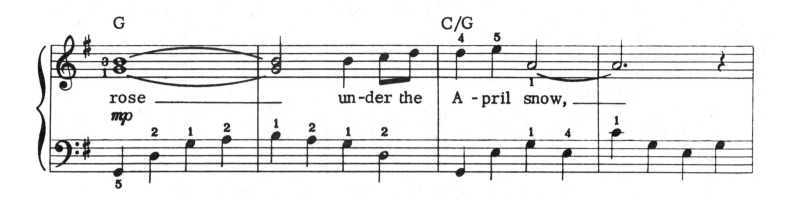

rose _____ un-der the A-pril snow, _____

I was al-ways cer-tain love would grow.

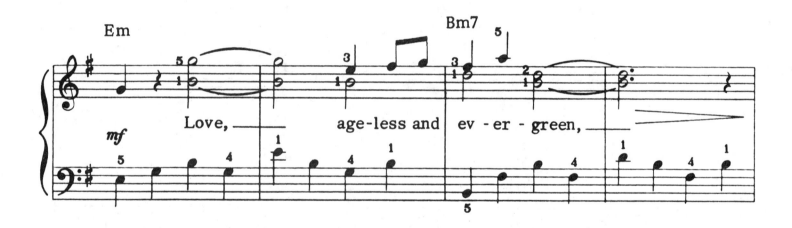

Love, _____ age-less and ev-er-green, _____

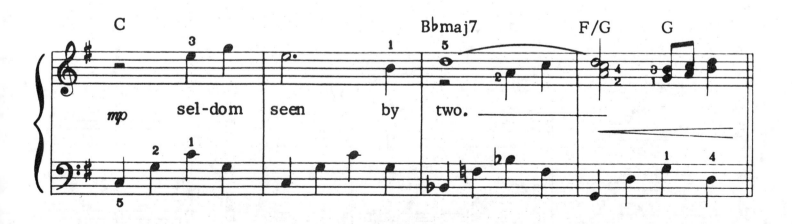

sel-dom seen by two. _____

FEELS SO RIGHT

Words and Music by
RANDY OWEN
Arranged by DAN COATES

Moderately slow

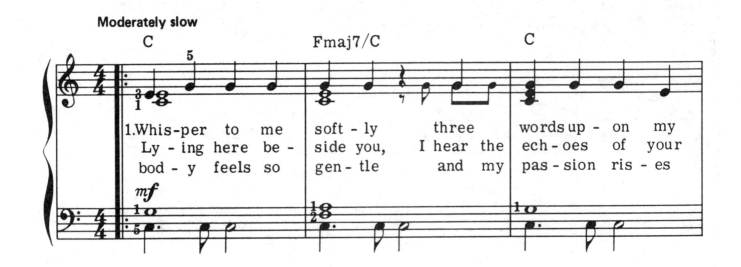

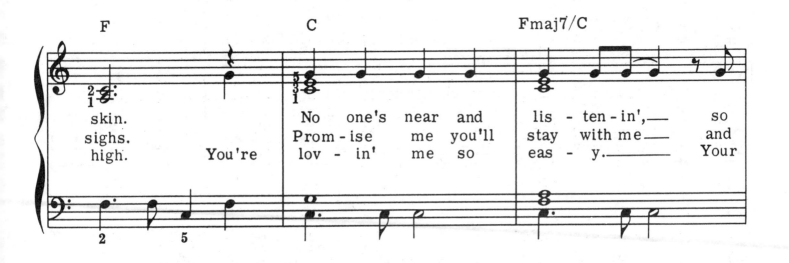

love me.___ Press your lips to mine.___
love me.___ Give my heart a smile.___
love me.___ Tell me it won't end.___ Mm,___

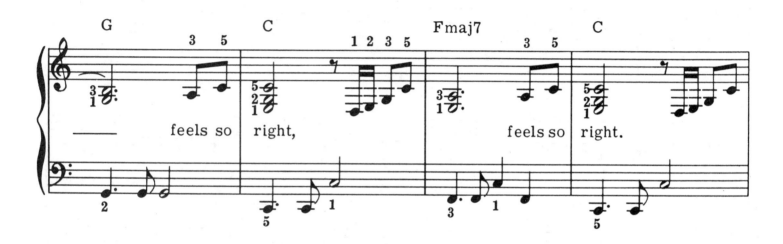

___ feels so right, feels so right.

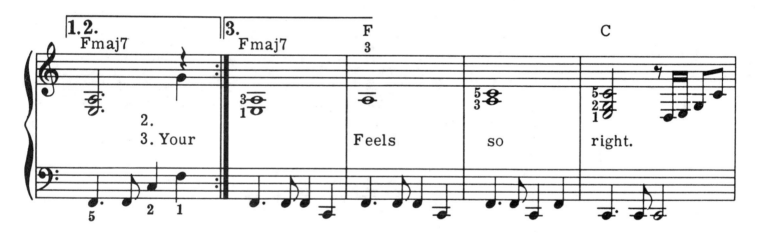

2.
3. Your Feels so right.

(spoken:) Aw, you feel so right, baby.

From the Broadway Musical "FIDDLER ON THE ROOF"

FIDDLER ON THE ROOF

Words and Music by
SHELDON HARNICK
and JERRY BOCK
Arranged by DAN COATES

Why should he pick so cu-ri-ous a place to play his lit-tle fid-dler's

tune? A fid-dler on the roof, a

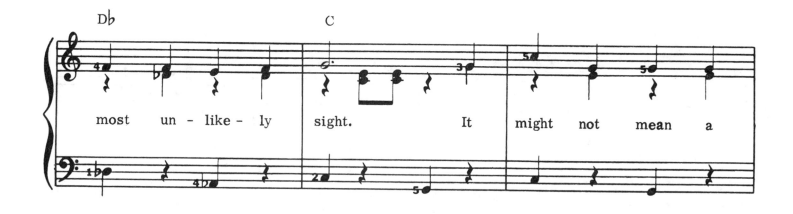

most un-like-ly sight. It might not mean a

thing, but then a-gain it might!

FORTY-SECOND STREET

Words by
AL DUBIN

Music by
HARRY WARREN
Arranged by DAN COATES

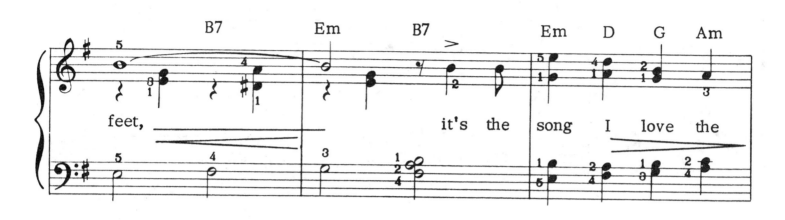

feet, _____ it's the song I love the

mel - o - dy of, ____ For - ty Sec - ond

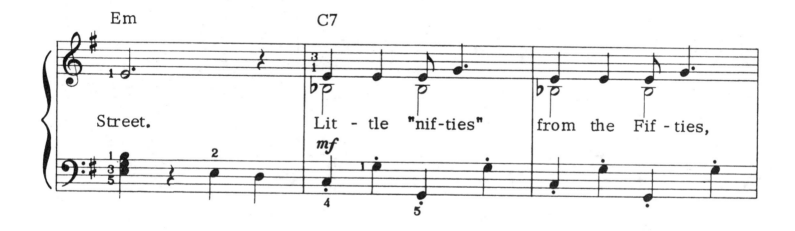

Street. Lit - tle "nif-ties" from the Fif - ties,

in - no -cent and sweet' sex - y la-dies

THE HIGH AND THE MIGHTY

Words by
NED WASHINGTON

Music by
DIMITRI TIOMKIN
Arranged by DAN COATES

HIGH HOPES

Words by
SAMMY CAHN

Music by
JAMES VAN HEUSEN
Arranged by DAN COATES

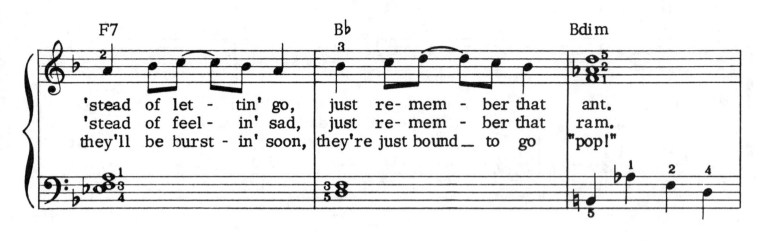

'stead of let - tin' go, just re- mem - ber that ant.
'stead of feel - in' sad, just re- mem - ber that ram.
they'll be burst - in' soon, they're just bound to go "pop!"

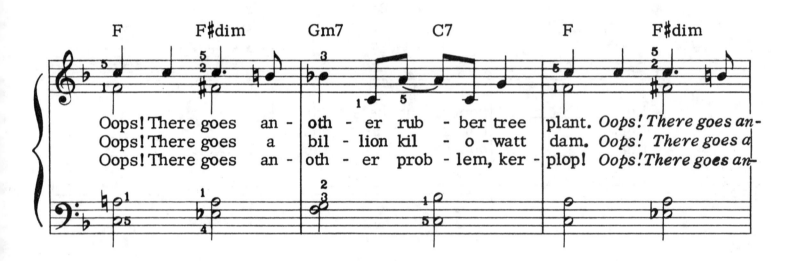

Oops! There goes an- oth - er rub - ber tree plant. Oops! There goes an-
Oops! There goes a bil - lion kil - o -watt dam. Oops! There goes a
Oops! There goes an - oth - er prob - lem, ker - plop! Oops! There goes an-

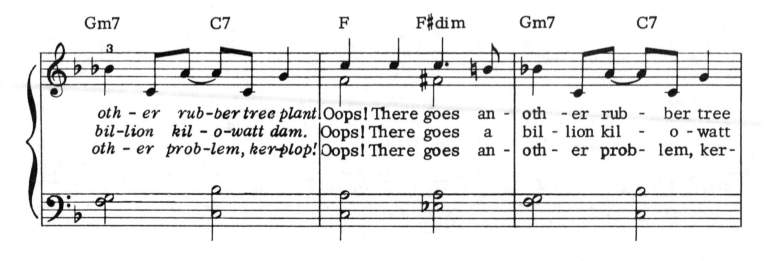

oth - er rub-ber tree plant. Oops! There goes an - oth - er rub - ber tree
bil-lion kil - o-watt dam. Oops! There goes a bil - lion kil - o - watt
oth - er prob-lem, ker-plop! Oops! There goes an - oth - er prob- lem, ker-

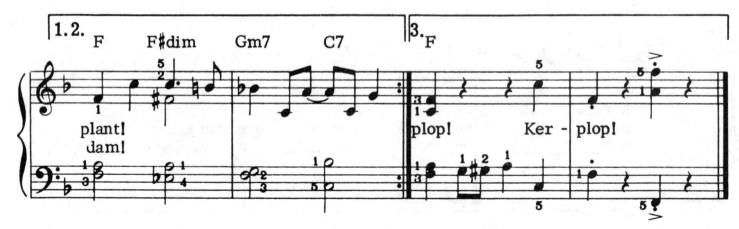

plant!   plop!   Ker - plop!
dam!

From the Warner Bros. Film "PURE COUNTRY"

I CROSS MY HEART

Words and Music by
STEVE DORFF and
ERIC KAZ
Arranged by DAN COATES

2. You will mine.

And if a - long the way we find a day

it starts to storm, you've got the prom - ise of my

D.S. 𝄋 al Coda ⊕

love to keep you warm.

Additional Lyrics

2. You will always be the miracle
That makes my life complete.
And as long as there's a breath in me
I'll make yours just as sweet.
As we look into the future,
It's as far as we can see.
So let's make each tomorrow
Be the best that it can be.
(To Chorus)

HOLD ME, THRILL ME, KISS ME

Words and Music by
HARRY NOBLE
Arranged by DAN COATES

91

THE HOMECOMING

By
HAGOOD HARDY
Arranged by DAN COATES

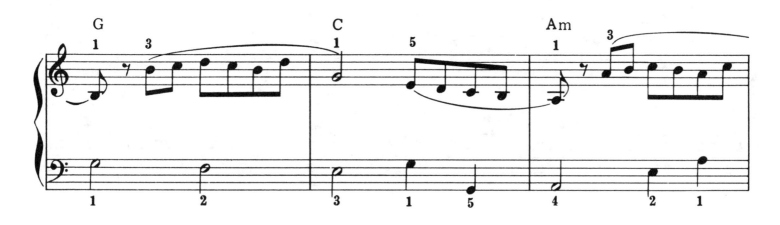

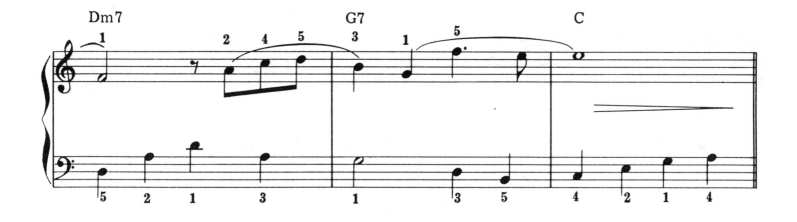

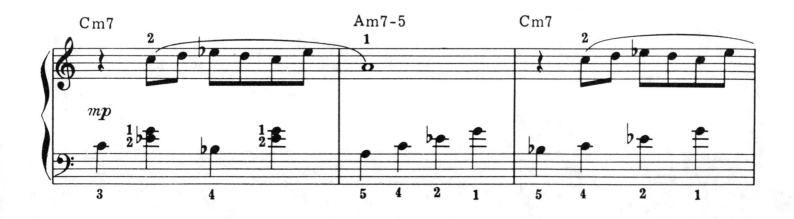

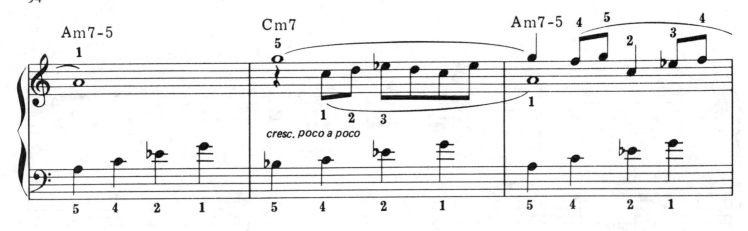

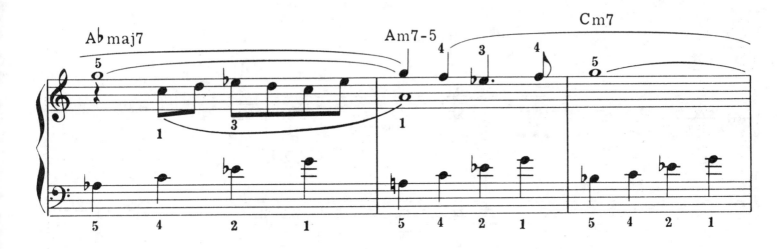

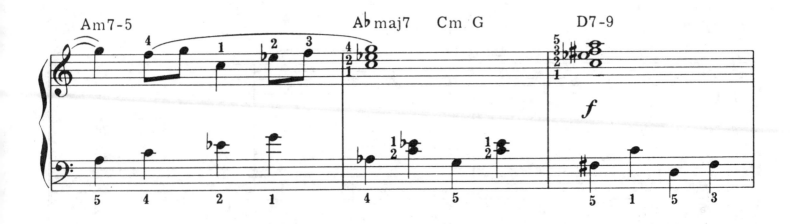

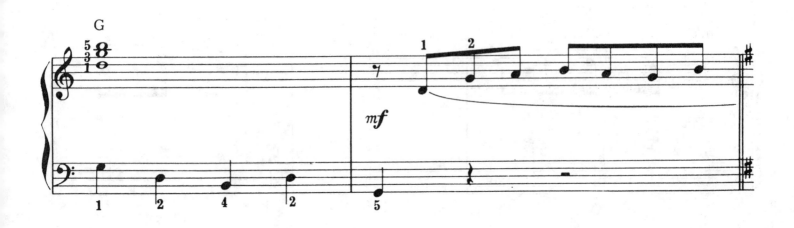

HOW DO YOU KEEP THE MUSIC PLAYING?

Words by
ALAN and MARILYN BERGMAN

Music by
MICHEL LEGRAND
Arranged by DAN COATES

I HAVE NOTHING

Words and Music by
LINDA THOMPSON and DAVID FOSTER
Arranged by DAN COATES

Moderately Slow

Share my life, take me for what I am. 'Cause
You see me, life through, right to the heart of me.

I'll nev-er change all my col-ors for you.
break down my walls with all the strength of your love.

From the Broadway Musical "FIDDLER ON THE ROOF"

IF I WERE A RICH MAN

Lyrics by
SHELDON HARNICK

Music by
JERRY BOCK
Arranged by DAN COATES

IT GOES LIKE IT GOES

Words by
NORMAN GIMBEL

Music by
DAVID SHIRE
Arranged by DAN COATES

KILLING ME SOFTLY WITH HIS SONG

Words by
NORMAN GIMBEL

Music by
CHARLES FOX
Arranged by DAN COATES

From the Film "THE PRIME OF MISS JEAN BRODIE"

JEAN

Words and Music by
ROD McKUEN
Arranged by DAN COATES

KARMA CHAMELEON

Words and Music by
GEORGE O'DOWD, JON MOSS,
ROY HAY, MICKEY CRAIG
and PHIL PICKETT
Arranged by DAN COATES

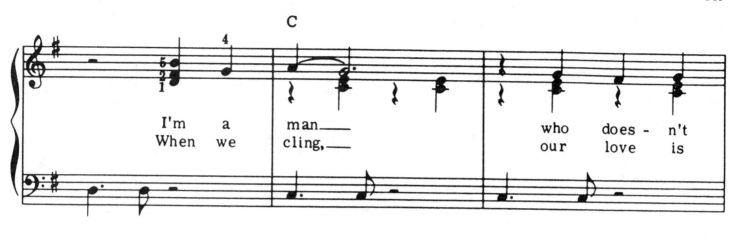

I'm a man____
When we

who does - n't
our love is

know
strong,

how to
when you

sell____
go____

a con - tra - dic - tion.____
you're gone for - e - ver.____

You come and.
You string a -

go,
long,

you come and
you string a -

go.____
long.____

Chorus

Kar-ma kar-ma kar-ma kar-ma kar-ma cha-me - le - on,

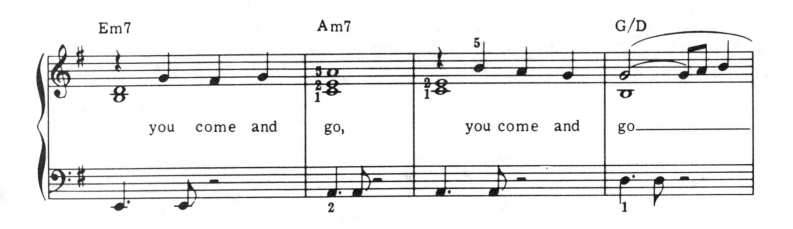

you come and go, you come and go———

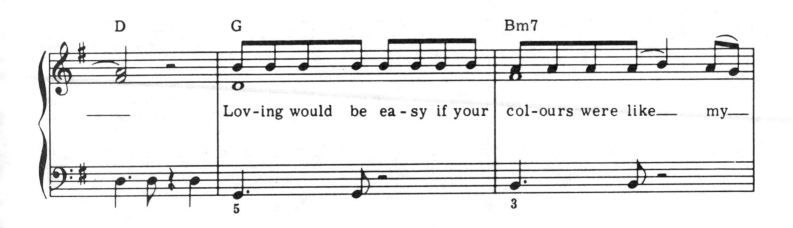

——— Lov-ing would be ea-sy if your col-ours were like—— my——

dream, red, gold and green, red, gold and

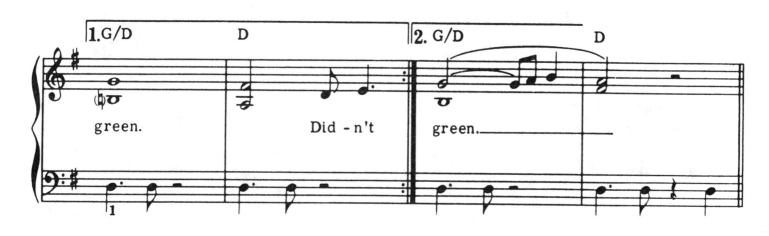

green.   Did-n't   green.

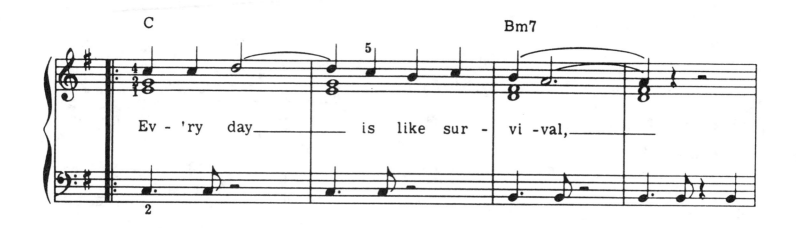

Ev - 'ry day_____ is like sur - vi -val,_____

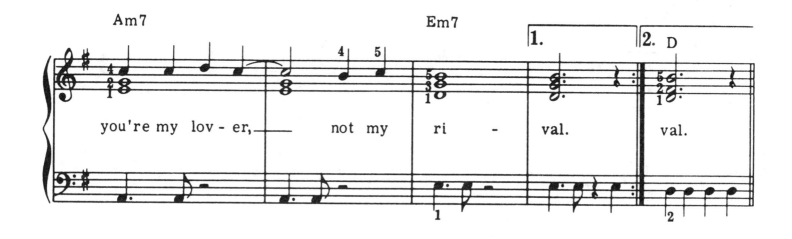

you're my lov - er,_____ not my ri - val.   val.

THE LADY IS A TRAMP

Words by
LORENZ HART

Music by
RICHARD RODGERS
Arranged by DAN COATES

Brightly (not too fast)

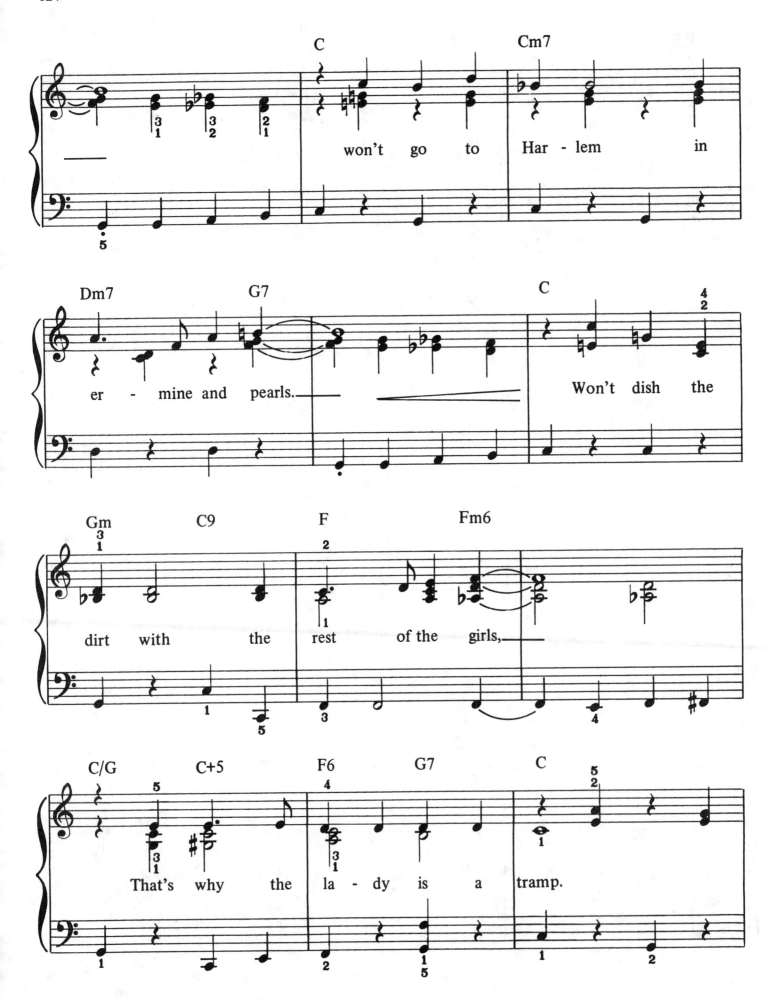

LULLABY OF BIRDLAND

Words by
GEORGE DAVIS WEISS

Music by
GEORGE SHEARING
Arranged by DAN COATES

And there's a weep-y old wil -

- low;____ he real - ly knows how to cry!____

____ That's how I'd cry in my pil -

low____ if you should tell me fare - well____

LOVE IS

Words and Music by
JOHN KELLER,
TONIO K. and MICHAEL CARUSO
Arranged by DAN COATES

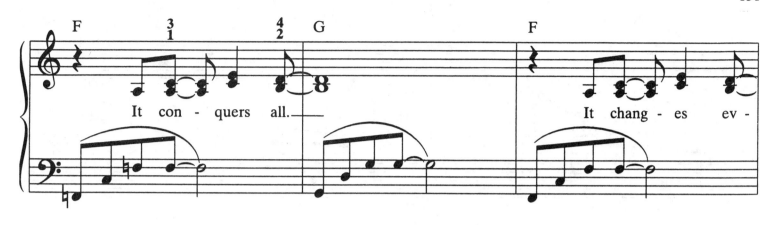

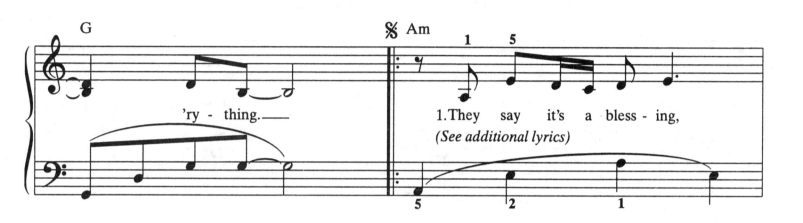

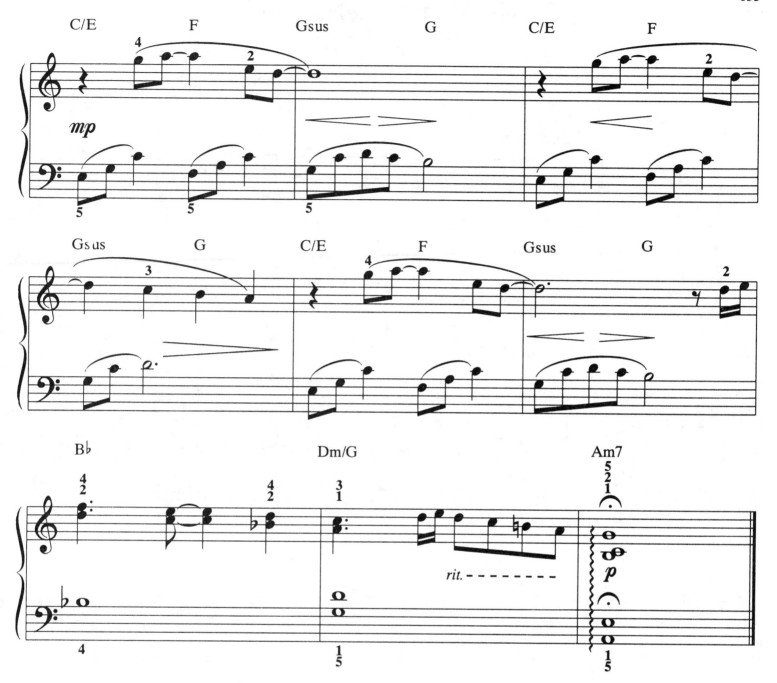

Additional Lyrics:

2. In this world we've created,
   In this place that we live,
   In the blink of an eye, babe,
   The darkness slips in.
   Love lights the world,
   Unites the lovers for eternity.

   Love breaks the chains.
   Love aches for every one of us.
   Love takes the tears and the pain
   And it turns it into
   The beauty that remains.

SONG FROM "M*A*S*H"
From the Film M*A*S*H

Words and Music by
MIKE ALTMAN and JOHNNY MANDEL
Arranged by DAN COATES

1. Try to find a way to make
   All our little joys relate
   Without that ever-present hate
   But now I know that it's too late.
   And -(Chorus)

3. The game of life is hard to play,
   I'm going to lose it anyway,
   The losing card I'll someday lay,
   So this is all I have to say,
   That -(Chorus)

4. The only way to win, is cheat
   And lay it down before I'm beat,
   And to another give a seat
   For that's the only painless feat.
   'Cause: -(Chorus)

5. The sword of time will pierce our skins,
   It doesn't hurt when it begins
   But as it works its way on in,
   The pain grows stronger, watch it grin.
   For: -(Chorus)

6. A brave man once requested me
   To answer questions that are key,
   Is it to be or not to be
   And I replied; "Oh, why ask me."
   'Cause: -(Chorus)

MISTY

Words by
JOHNNY BURKE

Music by
ERROLL GARNER
Arranged by DAN COATES

NINE TO FIVE

Words and Music by
DOLLY PARTON
Arranged by DAN COATES

Verse 2:
They let you dream just to watch them shatter;
You're just a step on the boss man's ladder,
But you've got dreams he'll never take away.
In the same boat with a lot of your friends;
Waitin' for the day your ship'll come in,
And the tide's gonna turn, and it's all gonna roll your way.
(To Chorus:)

Chorus 4, 6:
Nine to five, they've got you where they want you;
There's a better life and you dream about it, don't you?
It's a rich man's game, no matter what they call it;
And you spend your life putting money in his pocket.

THE MORNING AFTER
From the Film "THE POSEIDON ADVENTURE"

Words and Music by
AL KASHA and JOEL HIRSCHHORN
Arranged by DAN COATES

MY OWN TRUE LOVE
(TARA THEME)

Words by
MACK DAVID

Music by
MAX STEINER
Arranged by DAN COATES

OLYMPIC FANFARE AND THEME

By
JOHN WILLIAMS
Arranged by DAN COATES

*Bass Note Optional

From the TriStar Pictures Feature Film "ONLY YOU"

ONCE IN A LIFETIME

Words and Music by
WALTER AFANASIEFF, MICHAEL BOLTON
and DIANE WARREN
Arranged by DAN COATES

To Coda ⊕

shine with one rea - son, lead - ing your heart to the one love you find, just once in a

life - time. _____

life - time. _____ If you be - lieve in the pow - er of

love, _____ then you be - lieve that dreams come true. Mag - ic will fill your heart when that

PACHELBEL CANON IN D

By
JOHANN PACHELBEL
Arranged by DAN COATES

Slowly

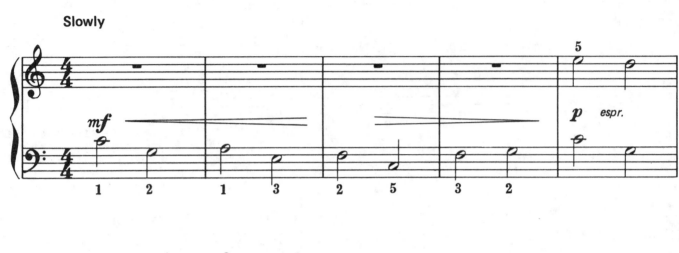

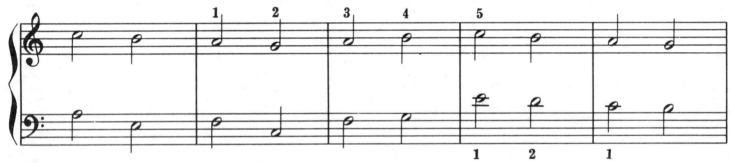

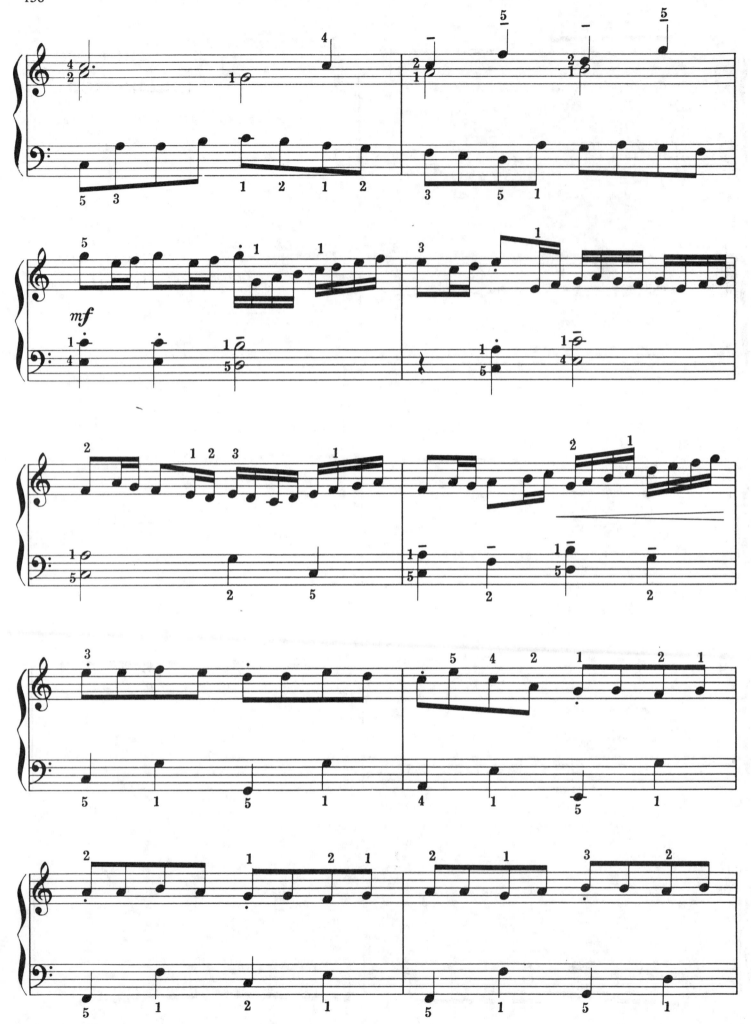

RHINESTONE COWBOY

Words and Music by
LARRY WEISS
Arranged by DAN COATES

2. Well, I really don't mind the rain
   And a smile can hide the pain;
   But you're down when you're riding a train
   That's taking the long way...
   But I dream of the things I'll do
   With a subway token and a dollar
   Tucked inside my shoe...
   There's been a load of compromisin'
   On the road to my horizon;
   But I'm gonna be where the lights are shinin' on me..
   (Like a)... (Chorus)

THE SWEETEST DAYS

Words and Music by
WENDY WALDMAN, JON LIND
and PHIL GALDSTON
Arranged by DAN COATES

RUNAWAY TRAIN

Words and Music by
DAVID PIRNER
Arranged by DAN COATES

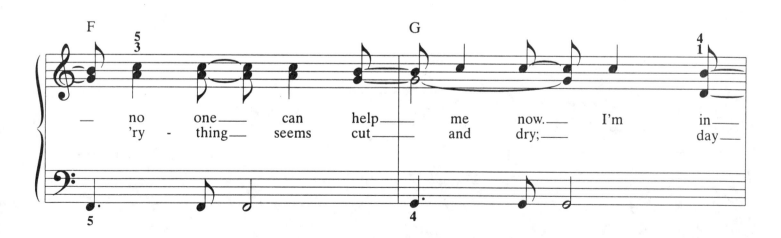

Bought a tick-et for a run-a-way train.— Like a mad man

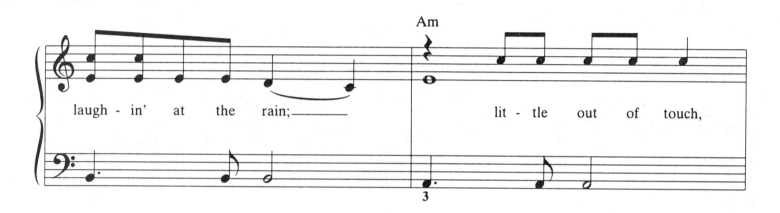

laugh-in' at the rain;——— lit-tle out of touch,

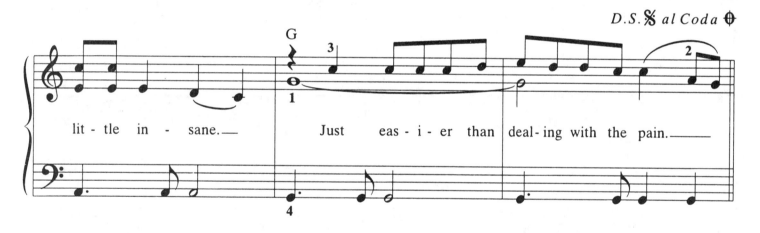

lit-tle in - sane.— Just eas-i-er than deal-ing with the pain.——

SEND IN THE CLOWNS
From "A LITTLE NIGHT MUSIC"

Words and Music by
STEPHEN SONDHEIM
Arranged by DAN COATES

A TOMMY VALANDO PUBLICATION

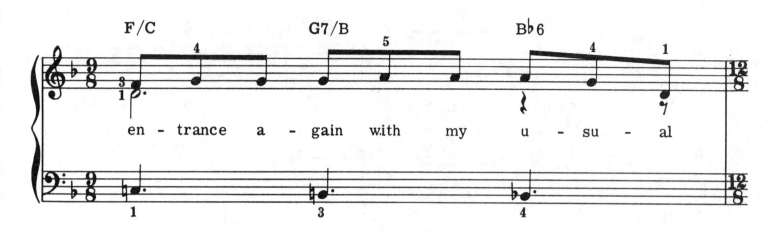

en - trance a - gain with my u - su - al

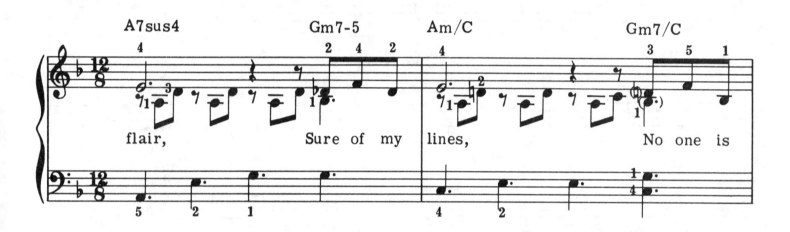

flair, Sure of my lines, No one is

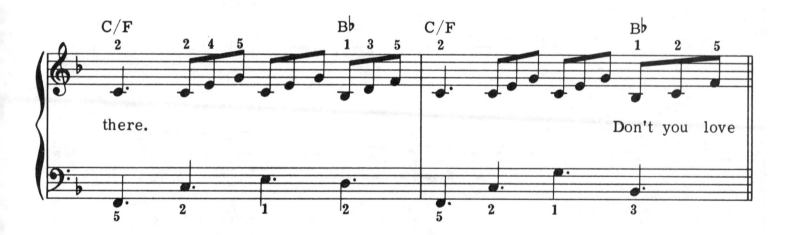

there. Don't you love

farce? My fault, I fear. I thought that
rich, Is - n't it queer, Los -ing my

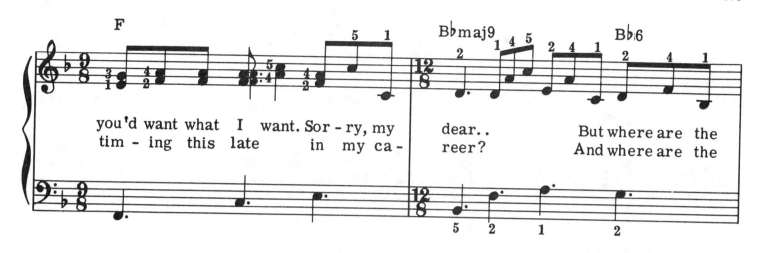

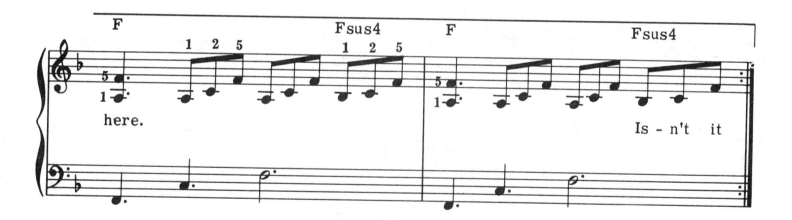

From the Broadway Musical "FIDDLER ON THE ROOF"

SUNRISE, SUNSET

Lyric by
SHELDON HARNICK

Music by
JERRY BOCK
Arranged by DAN COATES

2. Now is the little boy a bridegroom,
Now is the little girl a bride.
Under a canopy I see them, side by side.
Place the gold ring around her finger,
Share the sweet wine and break the glass;
Soon the full circle will have come to pass.
(To Chorus:)

STAR WARS
(Main Theme)
From the Films "STAR WARS" & "THE EMPIRE STRIKES BACK"

Music by
JOHN WILLIAMS
Arranged by DAN COATES

THE SWEETEST THING
(I've Ever Known)

Words and Music by
OTHA YOUNG
Arranged by DAN COATES

Moderately slow

From the Warner Bros. TV Movie "THE THORN BIRDS"

THE THORN BIRDS THEME

Music by
HENRY MANCINI
Arranged by DAN COATES

TIME IN A BOTTLE

Words and Music by
JIM CROCE
Arranged by DAN COATES

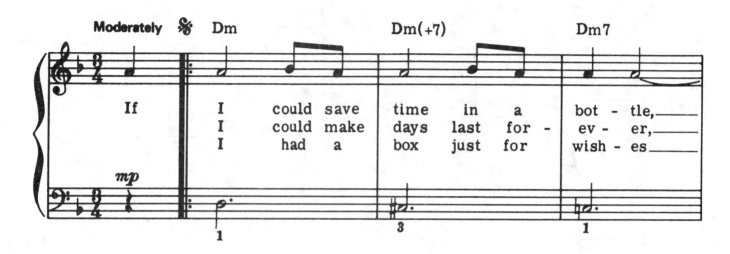

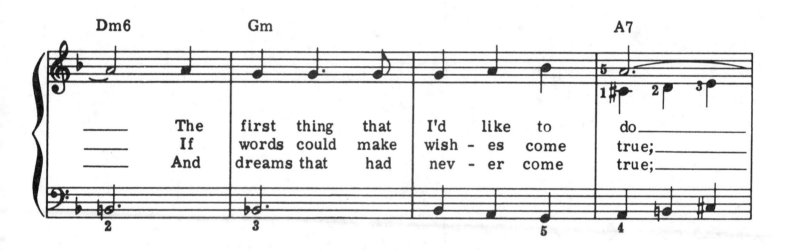

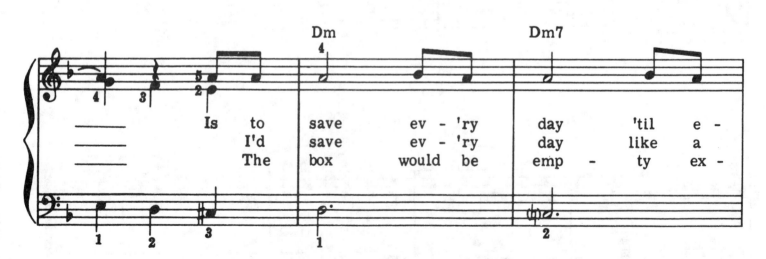

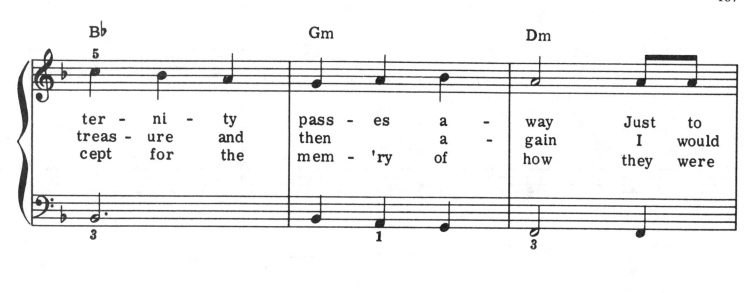

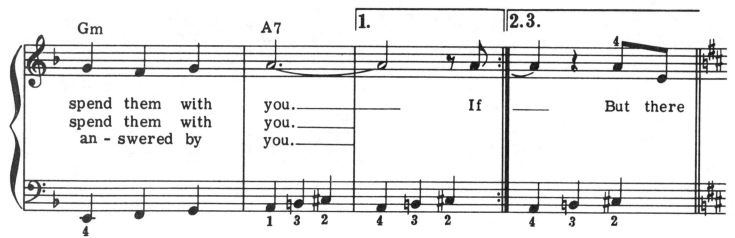

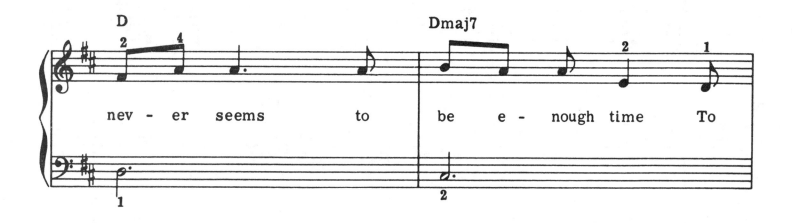

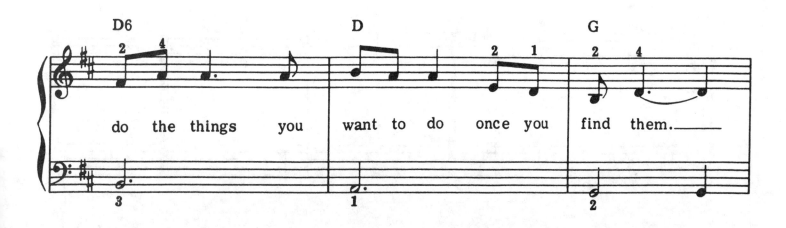

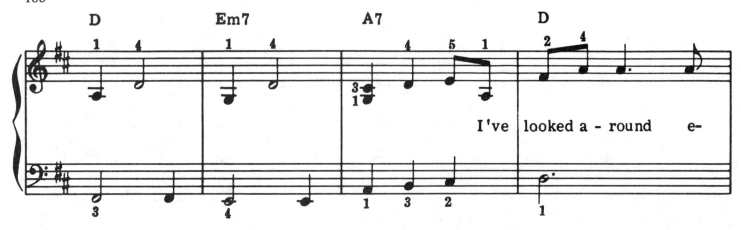

I've looked a - round e-

nough to know that you're the one I want to go thru

time with.

If

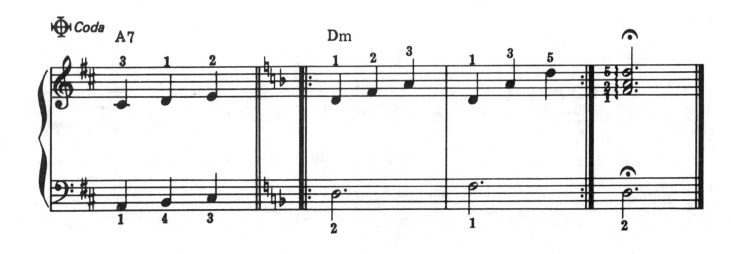

TONIGHT I CELEBRATE MY LOVE

Words and Music by
MICHAEL MASSER and GERRY GOFFIN
Arranged by DAN COATES

Slowly

Verse 3:

Tonight I celebrate my love for you
And soon this old world will seem brand new.
Tonight we will both discover
How friends turn into lovers.
When I make love to you.

WHAT'S NEW?

Words by
JOHNNY BURKE

Music by
BOB HAGGART
Arranged by DAN COATES

Moderately slow

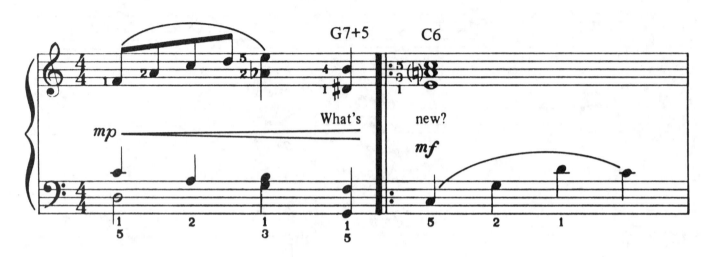

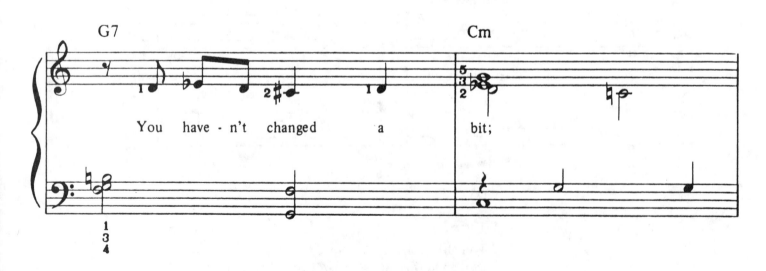

YOUNG AT HEART

Words by
CAROLYN LEIGH

Music by
JOHNNY RICHARDS
Arranged by DAN COATES

THE ROSE
From the Film "THE ROSE"

Words and Music by
AMANDA McBROOM
Arranged by DAN COATES

flow - er _____ and you _____ it's on-ly seed.

poco cresc.

It's the

heart _____ a - fraid of
night _____ has been too

mf

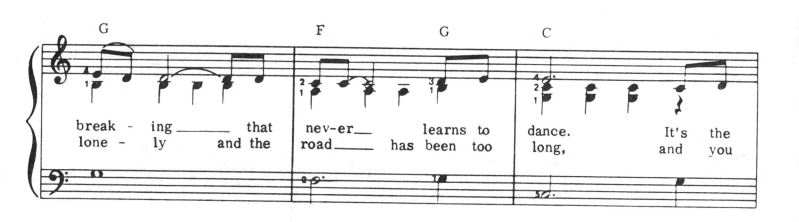

break - ing _____ that nev-er ___ learns to dance. It's the
lone - ly and the road ___ has been too long, and you

dream ___ a - fraid of wak - ing _____ that nev-er ___ takes the
think ___ that love is on - ly for the luck - y ___ and the

STAIRWAY TO HEAVEN

Words and Music by
JIMMY PAGE and ROBERT PLANT
Arranged by DAN COATES

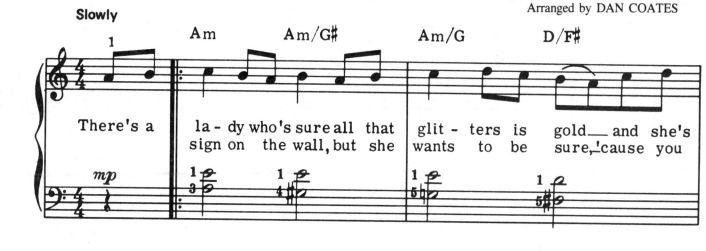

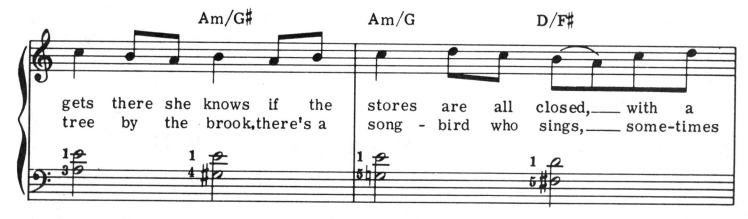

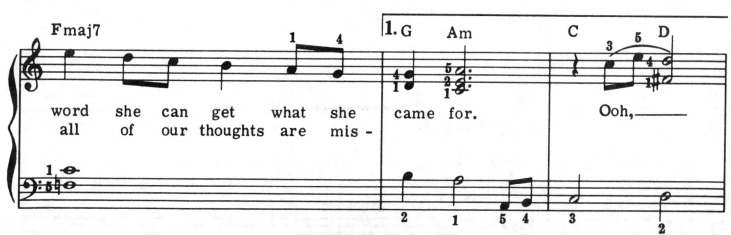

SAVE THE BEST FOR LAST

Words and Music by
WENDY WALDMAN, JON LIND
and PHIL GALDSTON
Arranged by DAN COATES

Additional Lyrics

Sometimes the snow comes down in June,
Sometimes the sun goes 'round the moon.
Just when I thought our chance had passed,
You go and save the best for last.

TAKE A BOW

Words and Music by
MADONNA CICCONE and BABYFACE
Arranged by DAN COATES

Take a bow,___ the night is o-ver, this mas-que-rade___ is

Make them laugh,___ it comes so eas-y when you get to the part___ where you're

THE DANCE

Words and Music by
TONY ARATA
Arranged by DAN COATES

I have known   that you'd   ev - er   say   good-bye?   And   now,_____ I'm glad I did - n't
who's to   say?   You   know I   might have changed it___ all.

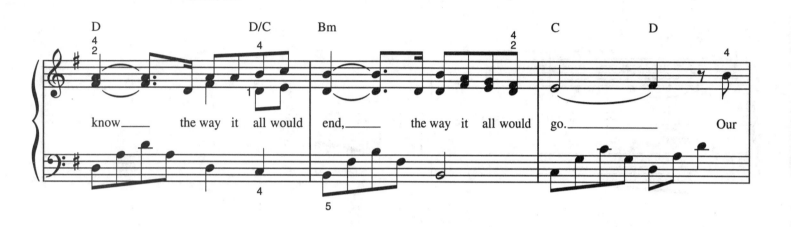

know_____ the way it   all would   end,_____ the way it   all would   go._____ Our

lives_____ are bet - ter left to   chance.____ I could have missed the   pain,_____ but I'd have had to

miss   the_____   dance._____   *mp*   2. Hold - ing

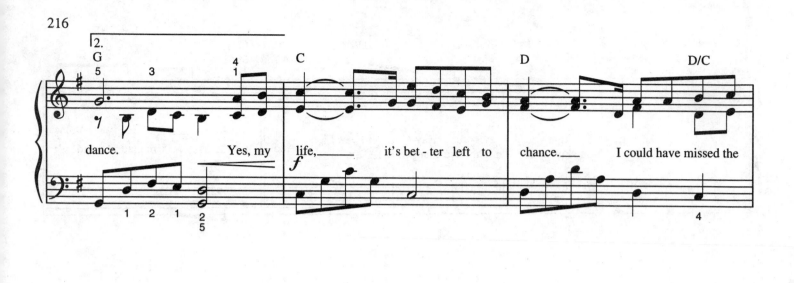

dance.   Yes, my   life,_____   it's bet - ter left to   chance.____   I could have missed the

pain,_____   but I'd have had to   miss   the_____   dance.

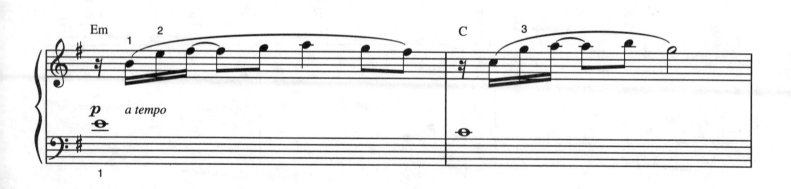

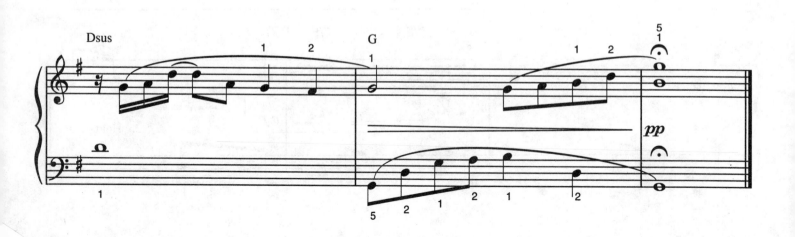